Planting

Seeds of Hope

DEE M RIVERS

Published by DMR
Cover design and Illustrations by Dee Rivers

This book has been created to enlighten the reader with observations of human nature and reflections on life. The stories and thoughts have been gleaned from the authors' life experiences.

Dedication

to my family around the world who have all
been part of my miracle,
the humble heroes of 2020
and last but by no means least, my sister
Veronica who I've known all my life as
Ronnie. You'll find her name threaded
throughout this book.

A message from Dee

April 5th 2020 is Palm Sunday, a day in the Christian calendar that celebrates the triumphant entrance of Jesus into Jerusalem. Triumphant, even though he arrived seated on a donkey, where an enormous crowd had gathered to welcome him with excited shouts of 'Hosanna'.

On this day in 2020, there can be no crowds, triumphant or otherwise. Only small close family groups are allowed to gather together. Thousands of people around the world are dying, sick, frightened and alone. We are in the midst of the worst worldwide crisis since the Spanish Flu erupted in 1918.

This is the year of the Corona Virus Pandemic. The world is thankful for the amazing gift we have in social media. The isolated need not feel isolated, the lonely need not feel lonely. Neighbours are helping neighbours and the list is endless of those working relentlessly, tirelessly to help the vulnerable.

I live alone and today am spending my time in prayerful contemplation, listening to Christian songs and hymns and watching my minister present his message via a video link.

There are no answers to the question, 'why'. There are no comforting words to offer. We don't know when it will end, but my friends, what I can tell you is this…Our Father in heaven knows the bigger picture. We are in his hands whether we believe in him or not. For me personally, I believe that Jesus Christ died for me on the cross and rose again to be with his father in heaven and that his Holy Spirit is our guide and helper in times of crisis and in times of joy. Without my faith, I truly don't know how I would cope with my life. I know that he is with me and is working out His purpose in all our lives.

I pray this little book will give you a shot of hope and maybe a respite from the worries of the day. Perhaps a fresh look at life will happen. You might find snatches of humour or events that you can relate to.

Please pray, if you can for help, for peace and healing.

May God keep you and your loved ones safe.

2020

Poppy for remembrance

When a Poppyseed falls to the ground it can stay dormant for many years, waiting for the best opportunity to begin it's push through the dark earth. Something in the ground will stir it into life or the climate has reached the perfect condition. Then the shoot will burst through to the light and blossom into that beautiful flower.

A word or a deed given in love to another person can become a seed planted in their heart. It might stay hidden for years leaving you ignorant of your part in their life. But God is caring for the seed, nurturing it until it is ready to sprout and grow. In time, the person becomes curious and questioning. The seed that you planted cannot contain itself any longer and bursts forth into the light of Jesus' love.

Acceptance of the love of Jesus becomes the beautiful flower that blossoms through their words and deeds. Thus, the circle of life continues as more seeds are planted in God's people.

Genesis: 1 v 29

Then God said, 'I give you every seed-bearing plant on the face of the earth and every tree that has fruit with seed in it. They will be yours for food.'

Snowdrop for beauty

Psalm 43:5b

Put your hope in God, for I will yet praise Him, my Saviour and My God.

The beauty
　　　of words...

Only fifty allowed!

Riding between the lines

Cycling to work,

riding between the double yellow lines

is like life,

full of pitfalls and hazards.

Swerve to the right, hit a car,

to the left, hit the pavement.

Watch for potholes and ironworks.

Guidelines disappear under parked cars.

Venture into moving traffic,

watch for pedestrians.

Arrived and safe!

Miracle on the internet

Are you sitting down?

I just received an email from our Aunt.

But we don't have any relatives.

We do now. Cousins all over the world.

Mum and Dad escaped their previous lives

to live together.

Dad, married with two children.

Mum, eldest of seven.

Suddenly we have a family.

Through my window

Grey clouds scudding this morning.

Gulls swooping, screaming.

Swallows darting across my view, whistling,

frantically chasing insects.

An aerobatic show.

Patches of blue brighten the sky.

Signs of summer.

Now the sun breaks through,

enlivens the day.

Rooks reel in the wind.

Seems before long dusk descends

and peace prevails.

A good story is like...

Afternoon tea on a windy day

Creamy soup after a bracing walk

A chat with close friends

A pick-me-up when you're down

A doorstep of bread and jam

A long cold drink in the sun

Fits of giggles

A comforting hug

A smile from a stranger

Hot chocolate with marshmallows

Sunflower for adoration

Psalm 113: 3

From the rising of the sun to the place where it sets, the name of the Lord is to be praised.

The glory of

Christian worship

His precious gift

Thank you, Jesus, for your precious gift to me,

So perfect, so pure,

Your Love, so freely given,

Too deep to understand.

Nothing in the world can prepare me

for a love like yours, Jesus.

No-one in the world can prepare me

for a love like yours, Jesus.

For yours is the love,

that takes me to the highest place.

Yours is the love

that leads me to the throne of grace.

Thank you, Jesus, for your precious gift to me,

So faithful, so sure,

Your love eternal,

Too vast to comprehend.

Thank you, Jesus,

for your precious gift to me,

So Holy, so true.

A love beyond compare,

Too real to fade away.

Lord, I give it all to you

Lord, I give it all to you,
my hurting heart, my painful memories.
I give it all to you, my doubts, my fears.

But sometimes I find it hard,
to let it go; to hand it over.
I hold onto my pride and go my own way.

Then you call me,
I can hear you, deep within my soul.
You remind me of your love;
How you've set me free.

Lord, I give it all to you,
my weaknesses, uncertainties.
I give it all to you, my life; my all.

But sometimes I find it hard

to let it go; to hand it over.

I hold onto my pride and go my own way.

Then you call me,

I can hear you, deep within my soul.

You remind me of your love;

How you've set me free.

Do you know how much God loves you?

Do you know how much God loves you?

Look around! Look around!

And you'll see Him in His gifts for you.

He's waiting patiently for you.

Wherever you should want to be,

the highest mountain, deepest sea,

He'll never leave you on your own.

Do you see how much He loves you?

Do you know how much God loves you?

Take it in! Take it in!

His love can be no more for you.

His love can be no less for you.

His love is perfect, freely given,

you only have to trust in Him

for everything your heart desires.

Do you see how much He loves you?

Do you know how much God loves you?

Do you know? Do you know?

He sent His only Son, for you,

to die upon a cross for you,

To take your sickness, needs, and pain.

To pay your debt of guilt and shame.

To buy your freedom with His death?

Do you see how much God loves you?

Do you know how much God loves you?

Close your eyes! Close your eyes!

And you'll hear Him calling out for you.

You'll feel His Spirit's touch on you.

He knows you deep within your soul.

His tender mercies make you whole.

He's chosen you to be His child.

Do you see how much God loves you?

Do you know how much God loves you?

Just believe! Just believe!

He only wants what's good for you.

He knows what's truly best for you.

Just call to Him and thank Him now.

He's waiting for you, call right now.

Just call to Him and thank Him now.

Do you see how much God loves you?

Jesus, you are always
on my mind

Jesus, you are always on my mind.
You are the one. You are the one.

You alone know my deepest thoughts,
even before I speak.
You have touched my heart with your eternal love;
much too deep for me to understand.

I'm walking on air with a spring in my step;
Your joy is filling my heart.
You have looked on me as your chosen one.
For my part, I just want to accept.

How precious to me are your thoughts,

Wonderful are your works.

Your presence is with me from dawn to dusk,

Your night is as bright as the day.

You heal my hurts and lead me in your way.

Jesus, you are always on my mind.

You are the one. You are the one.

Rose for love

Psalm 18: 1

I love you Lord, my strength.

A tribute

to parents

Mary the peacemaker

1997

This is a personal tribute to my mother, but will I'm sure, be acknowledged by many a son or daughter.

Recently, I had cause to remember an incident which happened when I was in my early teens. One day I arrived home from school to find that my mother had been rushed into hospital with shingles. She was never ill so this came as a big shock to me. I had no idea she had been suffering. My father was angry with me and announced (cruelly and unjustly, I thought) that I was the reason for her illness. I was very hurt at the time and the comment did not endear me to him. However, over the years I have come to realise that he was very worried about my mother and that was his way of dealing with the situation.

That is all I can recall about the incident but over the last few weeks, I have realized that indeed I could well have been the cause of my mother's illness. I was going through the typical phases of teenagers, discovering boys and wanting to do my own thing. In the normal run of things, this probably wouldn't have caused too much concern, but my mother had seen her young son growing up with behavioural problems and getting into trouble with the law. She's had to cope with being the peacemaker between my brother and father.

Now, as my children grow into maturity, I realize the fear she must have felt when I started to rebel. She must have been terrified I was going to go off the rails too. Yet there was never a word of recrimination from her towards me. There were many problems my mother had to deal with regarding my brother, not least was his sudden, accidental death at the age of twenty-one.

As far as I know Mum didn't have a close friend to talk to, her parents were both dead, so she must have kept all her feelings close inside her. My father was also a very demanding, insecure man. Despite all she had to endure, she was always there for us with rarely a cross word. When I think of how I often moan about not having enough time to myself or rush to talk to a friend when I'm low, I wonder how she ever stayed sane.

My respect for her as a woman is deeper now than I ever knew when she was alive. Is she one of a lost generation of women, committed to the family, keeping her chin up when all is crumbling around her; accepting her place in life without complaint? Mum worked full time with my father but was close beside us when my sister or I needed her.

Mum died about this time last year and I am learning new things about her all the time. But I guess I'll never know if she yearned to be free of her responsibilities; to have a close friend to let off steam to or just to have time to herself to do her own thing. I shall always be grateful to her for the incredible example she set, though I know I am nowhere near reaching her standard.

Unexpected answers to our questions

2019

I wrote that tribute to my mother over twenty years ago, not realising how significant my words in the last paragraph were.

Just two years later, (1999) my sister and I discovered life-changing truths that gave us a fresh insight into what Mum and Dad had been going through.

It hurts to say this. My parents had been living a lie for over sixty years. They had caused a scandal back in 1936, when our mother, a young Roman Catholic girl ran away with a married man who had two children. They changed their names and fled leaving behind her parents, four brothers and two sisters and his wife and children. They were never to see them again.

As was often the case in the 1950's children were discouraged from asking questions. But my sister and I were curious.

Discovering the truth gave us moments of anger but after the initial shock of finding that we had been part of their lie with a made-up name, we could understand more, our father's insecurities and why they supported each other through thick and thin. We also feel that Mum was plagued with guilt because of her actions, believing that the tragedies and trials they went through were her punishment.

For several weeks before her death, our mother had repeatedly asked for her Catholic priest to visit. She was dismissive of the kind-hearted ladies who came calling. I believe that she wanted to make her confession and her understanding was that only the priest would suffice. We have no proof that this happened, only that within three weeks of his visit, she had left this world.

Things my daddy said

For years, I believed every word my father said to me. No questions asked, his word was gospel.

These are some of them:

"There was a little girl and she had a little curl, right down the middle of her forehead. When she was good, she was very, very good, but when she was bad, she was horrid."

(Not written by my father, as I assumed, but by Henry Wadsworth Longfellow)

"Little girls should be seen and not heard."

(An early English proverb, probably dating back to 15ᵗʰ century)

"I'm going to see a man about a dog."

(As my mother was a breeder of dogs, this statement was always met by the plea, "Baggy me take it for walks. Promise!" The origins of this saying are unknown.)

"There was only one more like you, and she died coming across."

(I never did ask where she was coming from. The origins of this saying are unknown.)

"Eat your crusts, it'll make your hair curl."

(I was an adult before I did, and I have curls!)

"Eat your carrots. You'll be able to see in the dark."
(I did eat my carrots, but it didn't work!)

One time when I was in primary school, the teacher asked us all to find out our parents ages. When I asked my Daddy, he told me he was one hundred years old and I believed him. Of course, there was a smile from the teacher when I relayed this information and I became suspicious that she didn't believe me. On returning home, I innocently asked my mother, 'Daddy is one hundred, isn't he?' 'Don't believe everything your daddy tells you,' came her puzzling reply.

Growing up in the fifties, my siblings and I were discouraged from asking questions. Even as adults we didn't ask. It was as though we had been brain-washed. It was quite a common practice in those days. Family secrets were kept that way. And ours was no exception.

Violet for faithfulness

Matthew 21: 21,22

If you have faith and do not doubt......If you believe, you will receive whatever you ask for in prayer.

The power

of faithful prayer

A prayer for my child

Thursday, May 12th, 1998

Lord, are you in pain because your child is hurting?

Do you feel my frustration and pain, because the child you gave me to care for and to nurture is suffering?

A mother's greatest desire is for her child to be happy and well.

Are you suffering as I am?

But, you, O God have the power to change the situation.

I ask you now, in the Name of Jesus and all that is Holy; in the Name of the One who died on the cross, taking with Him our sickness and sin; in His Holy Name, please heal my child.

The one you gave me to love and to cherish.

Watch over us and bless us in your mercy.

Forgive me, Father, for ANYTHING I have done that is against your will.

Keep me walking in your WAY.

Have mercy on us.

Amen

Conversations with God

Prayer is a conversation with God. We can't see him, but he is there, listening and answering us. He wants to have a conversation with us. He didn't create us to be robots or puppets. He created us to have a relationship with him. A relationship needs connection. When we make a phone call on our landline, we can't see the other person, but when they reply we know they are there. God is not a computer voice. We don't need to press numbers to get in touch. And our Father is never too busy to take our call.

He loves to answer our prayers, but sometimes he can't get through to us. Our receiver is firmly down. There is no signal or we're too busy to answer, or we choose not to answer or it's inconvenient. As with any conversation, it takes at least two people. One talks while the other listens. It's an exchange. That's what God wants to have with us.

He wants us to answer his call.

The Lord's prayer

The Lord's Prayer is a blueprint for all our prayers.

Start by praising God that not only is he majestic and holy, but he is also personal and loving. He is our father:

> *Our Father in heaven, hallowed be thy name.*

Pray for the world in which we live, that all people will come to know God as their King.

> *Thy Kingdom come. Thy will be done on earth as it is in heaven.*

Pray for our daily needs, not just food but for everything that we need in our earthly life.

> *Give us today our daily bread.*

Once we've found forgiveness in our hearts for others, we can come to God with our pleas for his forgiveness

> *And forgive us our trespasses as we forgive those that trespass against us*

Ask God to help us recognize temptation and to give us the strength to overcome it.

> *Lead us not into temptation but deliver us from evil.*

We can be sure that God is supreme, so we should spend time worshipping God in the knowledge that his Kingdom will never end.

> *For thine is the kingdom, the power and the glory for ever and ever. Amen*

A teaspoon of prayer

God wants us to keep communicating with him. On a global scale, that is what's happening. All over the world individuals are lifting their voices to God.

Twenty-four hours a day, there is always someone speaking to God. When we're asleep, someone on the other side of the world is awake and praying. People have been praying throughout history. You can enter an old church and immediately get a sense of the prayers that have been said for hundreds of years.

It is easy to think that our simple, small prayer cannot possibly make a difference to world events, but someone once described this analogy: When we think our prayers are too small to make a difference, just imagine taking a teaspoon of water and tipping the water in a bath. Now imagine going back to the tap and repeating the action. You will need to repeat it many, many times but eventually, the bath would be full. Of course, you can always ask a friend or two to help.

That's what our small prayers are like. Continue to pray alone or, with two or three gathered together. You might not see the results, but down through the centuries, there have been men and women lifting up prayers for future generations – that is you and me. They could not have known how their prayers were answered.

Pansy for thoughts

Psalm 139: 17

How precious are your thoughts, O God! How vast the sum of them.

Home thoughts

from abroad

"Oh, the views!"

My sister, Ronnie emigrated to the USA in the early 1960s. She has often commented on the monotony of driving in the States; how a journey can continue for miles with nothing to see but an occasional tree or isolated farmstead.

On one visit she made back home to England, Ronnie suddenly had her eyes opened and was struck by things she hadn't noticed before. She remarked that whenever the road topped a hill, there appeared a fresh view for our delight. She was held in wonder at the winding country lanes that meandered through picture-postcard villages in Devon; in awe of the stone walls of the Derbyshire Dales that had stood for centuries; happily surprised by the colourful splashes of wildflowers in the hedge-rows and soothed by the pastoral sound of the bell tolling from a tiny rural church.

Having listened to my sister's enjoyment of our English countryside, gave me pause to think, am I taking it all for granted? I hope not.

Coming home

Whenever I travel home to Sussex after being away for a holiday, perhaps abroad or even within the UK, the view of the South Downs never ceases to take my breath away.

Travelling along the A27 or sitting on the train, as soon as the rolling hills appear, I know I am back home. I breathe a sigh of relief. There is the Long Man of Wilmington. Here and there I spot the sheep dotted on the hillside; walkers with their dogs bounding happily along the slopes. To my left are the hang-gliders, launching themselves off the highest peak, their colourful silks like giant butterflies swooping across the sky. What bravery!

There are many areas of Eastbourne where one can catch a glimpse of the Downs with their shifting shadows and ever-changing shades of green. Then, other days they mysteriously disappear in the mist. If a visitor came along on one of those days, they could be forgiven for not believing there were any Downs at all.

What a wonderful place to come home to.

Return to Wales

I was born in North Wales. On the day of my wedding, shortly before my twentieth birthday, I left home and to my shame rarely returned. I was embarking on a new life with my husband that did not include anything to do with Wales.

But on the first of those rare visits, I was shocked to hear that the people I knew, apart from my parents, all spoke with a Welsh accent. All the time I had lived there, I had never noticed that I was any different from the people I came into contact with daily.

I had always been quite a loner, finding it hard to make new friends when moving to a new school, of which there were several, so perhaps I stood out like a sore thumb with my English accent that followed my parents' way.

Primula for grace

John 1: 14

The word became flesh and made his dwelling among us. We have seen his glory, the glory of the One and Only, who came from the Father, full of grace and truth.

Amazing grace,

how sweet the sound

God's grace

The word 'grace' in worldly terms is a beautiful word. When we use it to define God's Grace it goes much deeper.

Grace is God's voluntary and loving favour given to those he saves. We can't earn it, nor do we deserve it. No religious or moral effort can gain it, for it comes only from God's mercy and love. Without God's Grace, no person can be saved.

Grace – the meaning of the word –

Elegance

Refinement

Loveliness

Kindness

Decency

Mercy

Charity

Clemency

Blessing

Goodwill

Grace – a verb –

To honour

To show favour

To adorn

To embellish

To enhance

To decorate

To dignify

Grace – in action –

A delay granted for payment of an obligation

Grace – a prayer –

May the Grace of our Lord Jesus Christ, the Love of God and the Fellowship of the Holy Spirit be with us all, evermore, Amen

For what we are about to receive, may the Lord make us truly thankful, Amen

Hail Mary, full of grace, the Lord is with thee; blessed art thou amongst women and blessed is the fruit of thy womb, Jesus.

Holy Mary, Mother of God, pray for us sinners, now and at the hour of our death. Amen.

Grace – a popular saying –

"There but for the Grace of God go I."

"My mother-in-law's Yorkshire puddings were her saving grace."

Grace – as a name –

Grace Kelly, a truly elegant woman who became a princess

Sharing the grace

The words in bold can be spoken in a group, aloud and with eyes wide open, sharing the Grace of God

The Grace of our Lord Jesus Christ. Lord Jesus Christ, through you we receive the Grace of God, that is – the unearned, unmerited kindness, mercy and forgiveness of God. It's wonderful, Lord that *we* know from your word that Your Grace is showered upon us, but many of the people in the world do not know this truth. Lord Jesus, help us to show them your Grace. The world has such a huge diversity of people, but thank you that you are always the same and you do not take into account any of our differences. Your Grace is for all of us in equal measure. Help us, Lord, to take your Grace to those people who do not yet know of it.

The Love of God. Amazing Love. What love is this that pays so dearly, that I, the guilty one, may go free? Those words, written by Graham Kendrick give a clear description of what you have done for us, the sacrifice you gave for us. We know Lord, that you give us perfect love and the love we have for each other is only possible through your Grace. Mighty God, we praise you and thank you for the ministers, the music groups, and all the people involved in running your church. Thank you for the many gifts that bring glory to you. Heavenly Father, as our love for one another grows, we pray that our gifts will develop and be used to further the work of your kingdom. Father God, we ask that you would help us to show your grace to all who come into our midst both familiar and new faces and as we share your love, so we receive more of your blessings. Dear Jesus, we thank you and praise you.

The Fellowship of the Holy Spirit. Holy Spirit, when we accept your fellowship with us, so we receive the Father's Love and the Grace of our Lord Jesus Christ. Let us open ourselves to the fellowship of the Holy Spirit as we begin to understand the depth of His love for each one of us. Thank you, Holy Spirit for your patient teaching and help. When we lose our way on life's journey you gently guide us on; when others let us down, you restore our confidence; when we stumble, you give us a helping hand; even when we are on our knees in the darkest pit, you bring us out into the light again. Knowing all of this, Holy Spirit we thank you that having fellowship with you is to have the Grace of God which is sufficient for all our needs. Holy Spirit, please teach us more of taking the Grace of our Lord Jesus Christ out into the community. Please teach us more about having the love of God for our brothers and sisters in Christ and please teach us more about having fellowship with you.

The words of a song by Peter Horrobin called, 'God whose son was once a man', seems very appropriate – 'Pour your Spirit on the church today, that your life through me may flow; Spirit-filled, I'll serve your name and live the truth I know. When the Spirit comes, new life is born, God's people share a bright new dawn. We'll heal the sick, we'll teach God's Word, we'll seek the lost, we'll obey the Lord, and it's all because the Spirit came that the world will never be the same because the Spirit came.'

Cyclamen for joy

Isaiah 55: 12

You will go out with joy and be led forth in peace; the mountains and hills will burst into song before you, and all the trees of the field will clap their hands.

Giggles

and laughter

Alien visitors

Someone visiting earth from another planet could be forgiven for thinking we are in agony when they encounter this phenomenon of giggling for the first time. They might see a person doubled over clutching their stomach, struggling to breathe, body shaking and tears rolling down their face with occasional strange noises issuing from their mouth or nose.

Uncontrollable bodily functions also feature in this strange behaviour. What's more, it is infectious. Before long a whole room will be engaged in the same torture. It can happen anywhere at any time: in an exam, in a church, at a funeral, while onstage or film-making, talking on the phone while cooking. The list is endless.

After several minutes, the visitor will be relieved when the human straightens up, has a little cough and a shake of the shoulders and begins to speak. Oh no, alarmingly, the behaviour starts all over again.

But, if the visitor asked the human should they call someone to help, we could truthfully reply that we don't need help, we are not ill or in pain. We are enjoying this best of feelings. I'm sure they would turn away with a puzzled shake of the head, while the whole process begins again.

Relieving stress or embarrassing?

Giggling relieves stress, nervous tension, embarrassment. It brings people together in ways other situations fail. No other earthly species has this behaviour. Some animals may show happiness or sadness, fear or joy, but not laughter. Giggling is laughter taken to the extreme.

When at secondary school, I once giggled my way through a maths exam as I sat at the back of the room. Needless to say, my results were not good.

Another time, when I was new to my school, the teacher asked me to join a line of pupils at the front of the class to read from a book. Yes, you've guessed it, I couldn't read a word as I became overcome with giggles.

Walking through town as a teenager one day with my mother, we were stopped by a lady who began to tell us about the death of someone they knew. I was suddenly overcome with embarrassment when my shoulders began to shake and I could feel a giggle bursting its way out of my mouth. Fortunately, I managed to turn away, almost hiding behind my mother. How terrible if the woman had thought I was laughing at her sad news.

My sister and I were on the way to a church we hadn't attended before. As we approached the building, we began to laugh for no apparent reason and once one of us had started, there was no stopping us. But we knew we would have to pull ourselves together before the door opened and we would be faced with the welcoming committee. We didn't dare look at each other throughout the whole service lest it set us off again.

My partner and I have spent many a time with only the sound of our wheezing while trying to bring our laughter under control during a telephone conversation. It can take just one word or an image to set us off. We are great gigglers.

To me, giggling is healing – a God-given gift.

Iris for wisdom and faith

Luke 2: 52

And Jesus grew in wisdom and stature, and in favour with God and men.

The wisdom

of God's word

Jesus the light of the world

Jesus said, 'I am the light of the world.'

Where there are dark places in our world of war, of suffering, of pain, of humiliation, of dictatorship
Lord Jesus Christ, please shine your light

Where there are dark places in our nation of greed, of all manner of abuse, of materialism, of denial of your existence
Lord Jesus Christ, please shine your light

Where there are dark places in people of division, of ignorance, of wrong teaching, of unscriptural living
Lord Jesus Christ, please shine your light

Where there are dark places in our city of poverty and homelessness, of crime, of neglect
Lord Jesus Christ, please shine your light

Where there are dark places in our lives of sadness, of jealousy, of loneliness, of sickness
Lord Jesus Christ, please shine your light

The Light of love shines in the darkness

Where there is your light, there is love.

Where there is your light, there is joy, peace and patience.

Where there is your light, there is kindness, goodness and faithfulness.

Where there is your light, there is gentleness and self-control.

Where there is your light, darkness cannot be.

Lord Jesus Christ, please shine your light

God's time-table

As human beings in the twenty-first century, we have become a society that belongs to the 'want-it-now' culture. We want fast cars, fast food, fast internet and even fast answers to our prayers.

A loved one is desperately ill; we want them healed – fast.

We want to know if we should take this or that job – fast.

We'd like a decision on an important difficult choice – fast

The list could go on. And anyway, we might think, God knows what we want before we ask for it, so what is the point in asking?

Let's remember that God is not a magician with a magic wand. He's not going to give us three wishes nor does he want us to reel off a shopping list.

His word says, 'Whatever you ask for in my name, you shall receive.' Note the words 'ask for'. Our heavenly Father yearns for a relationship with us. He has given us free will, so that we could make choices and to have choices we need to have communication with Him. By choosing to ask in prayer, we are choosing to have a relationship with our loving Father.

We have to learn to slow down, be patient. God's timing is not our timing. Sometimes he says, 'yes,' sometimes he says, 'no,' and sometimes his reply is, 'not yet.'

God's masterpiece

In Psalm 139 verses 13 to 16, the psalmist uses the imagery of God knitting us together. Verse 13 says, 'you knit me together in my mother's womb.'

In a piece of knitting, whether a scarf or an intricate lacy shawl, every stitch will show, giving it shape, beauty, and individuality. And that is exactly how God has created us each individually. He was involved in creating every aspect of our physique and personality – intricately, intimately, precisely. God made our inmost being, gave us our character, like and dislikes.

In verse 15 we see the words, 'my frame' and 'woven together.' This time the psalmist is using weaving as his imagery. There is a different method to create a woven piece of work. With weaving, as with cross-stitch and embroidery, a frame is needed to keep the fabric taut so that the threads are positioned correctly. The frame, the fabric, and the threads when worked together correctly will create a beautiful picture.

If we think of our bodies in the context of frame and threads – the frame being our skeletal structure – God saw us in our unframed state (that is the frame, fabric, and threads separate) and made us up exactly to the design he wanted, using the threads of DNA to give us the details of our make-up.

God's work is wonderful. There are no mistakes. God knew how your body would be affected by genetic inheritance, scars, and ageing. He set your body on its course. Nothing that has happened to you is unexpected to him. He has a purpose in everything he has decreed for you.

Knowing all this, we might be concerned about all the bad things that are inside us, putting God way down our list of priorities. How does that tie up with God's picture of us being wonderfully made?

If we turn a piece of embroidery over and inspect the back, there will be threads crossing, possibly some loose ends and knots. The picture that is so beautiful on the front is only a smudgy, jumbled image that we see.

So, on the inside, we are a bit like the reverse side of that picture, but God sees the finished picture, - his masterpiece.

If you've ever seen a breath-taking sunset and thought, 'Wow, isn't God amazing?' Verse 14 says, 'I praise you because I am fearfully and wonderfully made.' Looking in the mirror should take our breath away. All of creation is just a backdrop to God's masterpiece – humans, me and you.

God has a special name for me

Names are special. Our name identifies us, separates us one from another. Names have meanings. We read in the bible how God gave people new names. I wondered what name God might have given me. After spending some time in prayer, I came to this conclusion:

God's name for me is My Little Dove. I know this sounds fanciful, but bear with me!

One day I was gazing at my garden through the kitchen window, watching the sparrows and starlings jostling for position at the bird table. A shy collared dove was standing back, patiently waiting for her turn. After several minutes, it was as though she decided, 'Enough is enough, it's my turn now.' She pushed her way in and began to peck at the seeds furiously.

I realized that this dove's attitude was similar to my own. I don't like to push myself forward, but when pressed, I will make myself heard.

'My Little Dove' as God's name for me was confirmed when I went on a healing weekend. It was held in the beautiful setting of Glyndley Manor in East Sussex. We were eight ladies sharing a bedroom. My favourite place to wake in the morning is near a window with a view. The bed chosen for me was next to the window with a view of giant trees towering over the colourful garden.

God has chosen this position for me, was my first thought. With the sun streaming across the room, I made my way to the bed. I noticed a bookmark that had been laid on the pillow whilst putting my bag on the floor There at the very top was a picture of a white dove in flight. The message beneath said,

Dear Dee,

The Lord is my light and my salvation – whom shall I fear? The Lord is the stronghold of my life – of whom shall I be afraid? Psalm 27:1

My weekend proved to be one of immense healing, giving me refreshment and a deep sense of God's peace that passes all understanding.

Storms of life

In Luke 6 v 46-49 we read about the wise and foolish builders. As we read God's Word and put it into practice in our daily lives, we will stand firm, no matter what life throws at us.

In Matthew 8 v 23-27 we are told about the disciples' fear being relieved as Jesus calms the storm. Because of my fear of water, my reaction would probably have been similar to that of the disciples. Imagine their awe when the storm calmed. Putting our trust in Jesus despite what is going around us will give us peace.

Mark 6 v 45-52 relates the unlikely story of Jesus walking on the water. This is possibly one of those stories of Jesus' life that doubters have the greatest difficulty believing. For those of us who have faith in Jesus being the Son of God, we accept it as truth. It shows what we can do if we have faith. We can take a scary situation and ask our Lord to take us through our storms of life, or hard decisions we need to make.

Three golden rules

Romans 12 v 12 gives us three golden rules, not unforgiving rules that bear no relation to real life. These are rules that are set in our hearts.

If we can follow these three rules we are assured of our daily happiness.

Be joyful in hope. As Christians, we can be. We do not hope for earthly joy and happiness, we hope for God's kind and fatherly help in all the unexpected changes within this life. We expect God's help in those situations. So, we can be joyful in our hope of God's help.

Having that sure hope, we can also **be patient** in troubling times. Though the ways of the Lord sometimes lead us through dark and difficult places, we know that all things work together for good for those who love God. With hope then, why should we not be patient in those difficult times? Patience gives us the peace that passes all understanding.

If at times our faith grows weak and our courage deserts us, we can **be constant** in prayer, knowing that in His own time the Lord will hear and help. Jesus himself has commanded us to pray and has promised to hear us.

These three golden rules are not set by a demanding God, they are encouragements based on Christ's love shown when he died on the cross, taking our sins on his shoulders. Having His forgiveness through faith, we can follow him.

A powerful word

Think for a moment about the word 'yes'; of the many ways it can be said, of the many different meanings of how such a small word can portray your thoughts and actions. A small but immensely powerful word, causing great moments in history, both personally and globally.

In Exodus 4 v 19, 20 we read of Moses reluctance to say 'yes' to the tasks God had set before him. He made all sorts of excuses. God gave many instructions to Moses, and eventually, he got on with the tasks. He was in constant communication with the Lord throughout his life, seeking God's will before moving forward. Because of his 'yes' he was able to lead the Israelites to the promised land even though he did not live to see it himself. So, his 'yes' was a powerful word that shaped the Jewish nation.

Reading Matthew 4 v 18-22 we learn about the 'yes' of the first disciples. If they had grumbled about leaving their work or had gone home to discuss Jesus' request with their families, they wouldn't have had their place in history that changed the world.

In the Garden of Gethsemane, Jesus prayed, "My Father, if it is possible, may this cup be taken from me. Yet not as I will, but as you will." Jesus was pleading with his Father to relieve him from the suffering he was about to endure, but in effect, he gave his Father his 'yes'. It was the most powerful 'yes' in the whole of creation. Without his 'yes' we wouldn't know the love of our Father God. Jesus was and is that YES.

Tulip for passion and belief

Luke 23: 46

Jesus called out in a loud voice, 'Father into your hands I commit my spirit.' When he had said this, he breathed his last.

Family traditions

at Easter and Christmas

Easter...

In the lead up to Easter, the time we call Lent, when I was a teenager, my mother and I would always find something to give up. Something that we liked, that gave us satisfaction to be sacrificing. I remember one year giving up chocolate, but the one that has stuck with me ever since was to stop taking sugar in my tea.

Now years later, I have come to realize that it's not the giving up of things we enjoy that is important, but the reminding oneself of what a sacrifice Jesus made for us when he went to the crucifix. His was the biggest sacrifice of all time, giving us the freedom to ask for forgiveness for our wrong-doing.

On Easter Sunday mornings, Dad would prepare soft-boiled eggs for me and my brother and sister. The eggs had been laid by our chickens that morning. We would get to work quickly painting a face on the dark brown surface. Then, a sharp tap on the head (of the egg), remove the broken bits, hopefully, all of them, before the best part. Mmm! To see that bright yellow liquid sliding down the shell when we dipped our toasty soldiers in, was mouth-watering. Even now, over sixty years later, I still enjoy a runny egg with soldiers. This was our family tradition during the late 1940s and perhaps into the early '50s. I don't remember having chocolate eggs.

Also...

For me, going to church on Easter Sunday morning has to be one of the best days of the year. We've had the sadness of remembering Christ's sacrificial death on Good Friday and the glorious celebration on the following Sunday morning is in stark contrast. What joy it is to sing our traditional hymns, raising our voices through the roof.

He's alive, he's alive, he has risen!

Christmas traditions too...

Traditions in our family at this time of year, I remember most from childhood.

An idyllic time of staying up late to go to Midnight Mass and visits by Father Christmas. This remains a special event for me, taking me right back to sitting on a hard pew, cuddled up to my mother, tiptoeing to the nativity scene to spot the baby Jesus who had been placed that night in the manger. I was always in awe of the reverence pervading my senses.

My father would be waiting back at home in the warm kitchen with hot sausage rolls, mince pies and ginger wine that we would attack greedily. Then off to bed before the excitement of the morning when we would search in our pillow-cases for presents. There was never very much inside, but that didn't matter to my brother and sister and me. There was usually a book, an orange and maybe a chocolate Santa or coins and perhaps a scarf or a cardie that my mother had knitted. One year my dad had made wooden toys for each of us. Whenever I catch the smell of a freshly ironed pillow-case, I am transported back to that time of my life.

Another tradition that was kept going for sixteen years while I lived with my husband and children in Nottingham, was to have a glowing coal fire on Christmas day. We were fortunate enough to live in a beautiful old house with a 'real' fireplace and that one day in the year I relished the whole procedure of preparing the kindling, folding sheets of newspaper and choosing small pieces of coal before carefully placing them in the grate.

Then came the exciting moment of striking the match and lighting the paper. What a joy to watch the kindling and coal catching alight. Then to sip hot milky coffee while curled on the sofa in front of the hearth, with the dog at my feet and a good book in my hand. Quite often the book would be forgotten as I gazed into the flames, wondering whether it was time to put on more coal.

The downside to having a coal fire, of course, is that the rest of the house freezes. Just like in the old days when there was no other choice of heating the house. For that one day though, it was a delight for the whole family but we were always thankful that we could get back to central heating afterwards.

My second favourite occasion on the church calendar has to be the midnight service on Christmas Eve. The awesome presence of God is palpable. The peace of God that passes all understanding wraps its arms around me. To me, it is a holy, emotional experience

Lily for beauty

Psalm 89: 1

I will sing of the Lord's great love for ever.

The beautiful gift

of music

My testimony to music

I have sometimes used music to illustrate the ongoing chapters of my life.

I was a shy girl growing up in North Wales but I loved to play the piano, sing, and to dance. I was happiest with my music…

When you're smiling, when you're smiling, the whole world smiles with you. (i)

And…

I could have danced all night and still have begged for more. (ii)

In 1965, I was married in St. David's Roman Catholic Church in Mold, North Wales. With a new husband and babies filling my life, my attention to music and church drifted away. The recipe for my life was set for the future as far as I was concerned…

One man, one wife, one love through life.
Memories are made of this. (iii).

About twenty years, several house-moves and four children later, we packed our belongings and settled in Nottingham. It was like coming home for me. I made friends with some wonderful ladies who introduced me to Jesus Christ. They shared with me how God is a loving father, not the scary, raging spirit waiting to strike us, that I understood and feared…

Amazing Grace, how sweet the sound, that saved a wretch like me.
I once was lost but now I'm found, was blind but now I see. (iv)

With the revelation of finding my faith again, I wrote this song to Jesus…

This is my love song to Jesus.
This is my love song to my Lord.
You are the one Lord, I treasure,
you are the One I adore.

Yes, you are the one, who has touched my heart,
with your eternal love.
Yes, you are the one, who knows my deepest thoughts,
yet you still love me.

This is my love song to Jesus.
This is my love song to my Lord.
You are the one Lord, I treasure,
you are the One I adore.

Yes, you are the one, who has set me free,
by dying on the cross.
Yes, you are the one, who gives me joy each day.
Jesus, I love you. (v)

For several years my marriage had been rocky, and in 1999, we separated, but with many hours of prayer, after six months, I moved back to my husband. I firmly trusted that God wanted me back in the family home.

I wanted to believe again that...

Love and marriage go together like a horse and carriage. (vi)

By 2003, my husband and I made the difficult choice to move South to be near our daughter. Very quickly our relationship hit rock bottom again. In the depths of despair, devastated that we were going over old ground that I thought had been dealt with, I lost the will to live. For my sanity and with a strength that could only come from God, I walked out of my forty-year marriage for good.

Suddenly I was free to be myself, the person God wanted me to be. I bought a piano and began to find my music again, playing in care homes for the elderly. I made good friends in the church, joining the music group and a local choir...

The hills are alive with the sound of music. (vii)

Composers:

i	*M Fisher, J Goodwin, L Shay*
ii	*A J Lerner, F Loewe*
iii	*T Gilkyson, R Dehr, F Miller*
iv	*Traditional*
v	*D Rivers*
vi	*S Cahn, J Van Heusen*
vii	*R Rogers, O Hammerstein*

Music in life

If we think of music as an analogy of life, you could say that before Christ, mankind was in discord with God. In the same way, we can look at our own lives. If we haven't accepted Jesus into our lives we are actually in disharmony with God. It's all on account of sin that the music that is our lives is out of sync with God's will.

The words we sing and the music we make, wonderfully teach us that this tuneless tumult has been ended because of Jesus. He has restored the harmony between God and humankind by his redemptive work on the cross.

The message of the Gospel causes us to exalt with full-throated joy. It produces in us an ever-increasing crescendo of praise and thanksgiving. The people of God sing with their hearts, mouths, and lives.

There is a time and place for a variety of styles of music – quiet reflection, ecstatic rejoicing, ancient favourite hymns and thankful praising; harmonies, chants, a cappella and tongues.

Blessed are those who are tolerant of those who are different from themselves.

Blessed are those who are bold in their adoration of the Lord.

.

Chrysanthemum for resignation and goodbye

Luke 23: 46

Jesus called out in a loud voice, "Father, into your hands I commit my spirit." When he said this, he breathed his last.

Unexpected emotions

On May 31st 2019, while I was in America visiting my sister, I received a phone call from my eldest son telling me that my ex-husband, their father had died that morning after several months of chronic asthma. He had not been an easy man to live with, suffering as he did from Bipolar disorder. We had been divorced for thirteen years and, though initially, we tried to keep some semblance of a relationship, that proved too difficult, thus we had not been in contact for several years.

I was shocked at my emotions when hearing the news of his passing. It was as though I was dreaming. When my family had told me earlier in the year that he was deteriorating, and on oxygen, my first thought was that he would rally round. I had seen him many times struggling with his breathing when a hefty dose of steroids soon had him back to his old self. But not this time.

Our four adult children got together, initially sorting through his possessions, their emotions playing havoc as each one of them called to mind his actions and behaviour towards them. They had been visiting him throughout the previous months, taking him to doctors and hospital appointments, helping to sort out care at home, often with little encouragement or thanks.

As ever, he was a stickler for doing what he wanted and, refusing to take the doctor's advice, remained in his home and that is where he died.

Once the apartment was emptied, the task of arranging his funeral was upon them. Our sons and daughter worked hard as a team to bring all their father's good points together with words and music, in what was a service I hope he would be proud of. Our daughter told me of the music they had chosen to play during the funeral service. It broke my heart to hear titles that had meant so much to us through our marriage. I was filled with sadness for what we had lost and what we might have had.

On the 20th June 2019, my entire family consisting of my daughter, three sons, two granddaughters and three grandsons gathered in Sutton Coldfield for the funeral. For many reasons, I decided that it would be best to stay home. Instead, I would be with my family in spirit and went to sit in a quiet spot in a beautiful park.

Later I took myself to the beach. The tide was out, so it was a long stony walk down to the water's edge. I stood for a while watching the waves lapping the shore, then turned to face the high mountain that I had to climb to reach the promenade. As I struggled across the pebbles, it reminded me of the years I had battled with my insecurities, and the terrible torment I went through before deciding to leave the life I had with my husband. Reaching breathlessly to the top gave me a sense of relief not too far removed from the same feeling on my first day of freedom. A freedom that was tinged with regret for what might have been.

The passing of parents

My parents ended their days while living in America. I had visited them both within the previous twelve months. Leaving them at the airport was heartbreaking, knowing that it would be the last time I would see them. In those days I didn't have the funds to travel back and forth between the UK and the US so even thinking of returning for their funerals was impossible.

They died about eight years apart and I so well remember the phone calls from my sister. My father was the first to go and his death didn't hit me until I went to the florist to order flowers for his funeral. Wanting to write a message on the card, I broke down and had to leave the shop until I had collected myself. For my mother, her funeral was only about three days after her death, so I couldn't have made it in time. She died on my youngest sons tenth birthday and was buried on my sister's birthday. Such sad times.

Daffodil for happiness

1 John 1: 3b, 4

And our fellowship is with the Father and with his Son, Jesus Christ. We write this to make our joy complete.

Silly things we do

that make us smile

Moon-crater cakes

I was especially proud of my new saucepans. They were the very latest in technology, so the salesman told me. I would be able to use them in the oven as well as on the hob. Boiling and baking were their 'thing'.

With the lid on, I could bake a cake, so this I set out to do. It seemed fool-proof. What could possibly go wrong?

With my first attempt taken carefully from the oven, I removed the lid. The cake popped out of the pan beautifully, but it was rather pale, with small craters dotted across the surface. This was caused by condensation dripping from the lid. I had done everything the salesman had told me to do but sadly the few times I attempted to bake cakes in this way resulted in the family erupting into gales of laughter and calling them Mum's 'moon-crater' cakes. The craze didn't last long as even I could see this method of baking cakes just wasn't successful.

Blackberry and apple pie

Many years ago, when I was a relatively new wife and mother, my husband decided to set off in search of blackberries while I prepared the pastry and apples to make a blackberry and apple pie, one of our favourite dishes. Again, what could possibly go wrong? I had used the recipe several times by then and felt rather confident.

The pastry and apples were all prepared by the time he arrived home, rather hot and scarred but proudly holding a bowl full of delicious-looking, glossy blackberries. I carefully washed them, inspecting for 'groddy's' before mixing them with the apples and a generous helping of sugar. The oven had reached the correct temperature and soon I was sliding the pie dish inside. The timer was set, so we ate our meal with the anticipation of a mouth-watering dessert.

I was so proud of my creation as I placed it in the centre of the table. The custard was there, steaming hot. I had followed the instructions on the packet so there was nothing to be hesitant about. I cut a generous slice for my hubby and one for myself before pouring on the thick bright yellow custard. I could see my husband's eyes glowing; he was looking forward to tasting the fruits of his hard-fought pickings.

As he pulled the spoon from his mouth, he let out an almighty roar. I dropped my cutlery, sending custard and pie across the table and onto the floor. What on earth had happened?

"What have you done?" he spluttered, as bits of pastry scattered over his jumper.

"I don't know. What's the matter?" I ventured.

What I had done was to add a generous helping of salt to the custard rather than sugar. Thank goodness it wasn't in the pie. At least we were able to enjoy the rest of it during the week. I made sure I didn't make the same mistake again!

Watery gravy

People could be forgiven for accusing me of being overly fussy about my gravy. It has to be a rich brown colour and not watery, preferably made with the juices of roast meat or vegetable stock. The consistency should be about the same as custard.

I had served up the dinners with the gravy ready in the gravy boat, but when the gravy was poured it was like dishwater.

How had it happened? I knew I had used vegetable stock, seasoned and thickened it in my usual way, so this was a mystery.

Later that night, I suddenly had a moment of realization. To keep the gravy hot when it was put into the gravy boat, I had partly filled the jug with hot water from the kettle. Then with all the dishing up and taking the plates to the table, I had forgotten about the water and added my lovely gravy to it.

Missing gloves?

On one occasion I had cause to complain that I couldn't find my gloves. I had prepared to go out with my coat, hat and scarf to keep me warm, but my gloves were not in their usual place. I fumbled in my handbag, not there. Inspected my flat, (just to mention, I have a studio flat so that didn't take long). No sign anywhere there. By this time, I was becoming very hot, wearing all my outdoor gear, as I was.

Ah, I must have left them in the car. Yes, that's the answer. I trooped outside, finally cooling down as I moved into the frosty air. A search in the car revealed only a pair of sunglasses, but I didn't need those, although I had been looking for those recently when there was a bright low sun. No, I was having no success.

Where could they be? Well, I'll just have to keep my hands in my pockets. With all the bending down to search inside the car, my hat had become slightly skewiff. I reached to pull it back into shape and realized that it had morphed into a rather bulky nature. Pulling the hat off to inspect it, I found the culprit – yes, you've guessed it. My gloves – placed inside my hat for safekeeping instead of putting them in their usual home.

Winged seeds for messengers

Malachi 3: 1a

See, I will send my messenger, who will prepare the way before me.

Do angels

exist?

My personal angel

Some years ago, I had booked a flight to visit my sister for Christmas in Ohio. The weather was atrocious with many flights cancelled. In freezing conditions, I arrived at the airport to find hundreds of passengers standing in a snaking queue of such magnitude that I had never witnessed before in all the years of my travelling to the States. In addition to the queue, there were hordes of people lying on the floor and benches surrounded by baggage.

I joined the end of the line, setting my large suitcase on the floor beside me before searching for a departure board. My head reeled when I discovered that my flight was one of only two that was scheduled to leave. I checked my boarding pass and saw that the number was correct and definitely mine. But what was I to do? The line shuffled forward a couple of steps.

After what seemed like a lifetime of shuffling, I had only moved about a metre. Whenever I glanced at the board, the time had inched toward boarding time and I was getting nowhere.

Unexpectedly, a woman in a navy blue, full-length coat appeared at my side. Looking straight at me, she asked which flight I was using. As soon as I pointed out the dilemma I was in, she grabbed my suitcase and shouted for me to follow her. By-passing all the waiting passengers, we arrived breathlessly at the check-in desk. She heaved my suitcase onto the conveyor belt and stood aside for me to follow the procedure. I turned to thank the lady, but she had completely disappeared.

By this time, the clock was ticking, the call for boarding had long gone. The next thing to do was to reach security. It looked a mile away. I would have been at home in a hurdle race as I dodged people and suitcases in my effort to hand over my boarding pass. My troubles weren't over yet. The pass wasn't accepted, which meant going to another desk while the security man contacted the flight staff that I was on my way. Back and forth between the desks, I ran as my boarding pass continued to deny its existence. Finally, I had the go-ahead to move through security.

Yanking my coat and shoes off, one sock came off too in my efforts to speed things up. The woman officer anxiously informed me that the plane was about to take off. At that point, images of miles of trekking ahead filled my mind, but bundling everything in my arms, I ran with one bare foot, almost colliding with a kind man who directed me down a flight of stairs to be met with….What?...I couldn't believe it…another queue of people. They hadn't all boarded yet. I got my breath back put my sock and shoes on, found my seat and was on my way. Phew, what a relief.

As the plane descended through the clouds towards Chicago, I could see a smattering of snow. This was my change-over airport so I needed to check my luggage and find the departure area. There was no rush. I had a couple of hours to spare so having done all the necessary procedure I ambled through to the lounge. My breath was knocked out of me with what I saw through the massive window. A snowstorm had blown up and several inches of snow had covered the ground. I watched as the airport staff drove monster snow ploughs towards the runways. Was I ever going to get to Detroit in this weather? I found a seat and sipped hot coffee while watching the worsening scene outside. By now the light had faded into darkness and I felt little hope of reaching my destination where my sister and brother-in-law would be anxiously waiting. There was no way to contact them.

As the time came closer for boarding, hopeful passengers began congregating in front of the departure board. I joined them feeling despondent at the thought of a night spent on an airport bench, and then what? What if planes were grounded for days? And so, my thoughts went on. Suddenly, there was a rush of movement and I was propelled within a mass of bodies all making for the boarding gate. Our plane was due to take off in half an hour. I didn't dare look out of the window at the weather. Surely, the ground staff hadn't been able to clear the runway with that blizzard gaining weight. But miraculously they had cleared enough for our flight to get off the ground. I was soon on the last leg of my eventful journey.

On arrival in a snow-covered Detroit, I found my sister and brother-in-law. They had been fearful for my safety as they had heard that a plane that was full of passengers and due to fly from Detroit to Chicago had been cancelled with all those on board being deposited back in Detroit airport. My flight was the last plane out of Chicago that night.

Without the help of the lady in the navy-blue coat at Heathrow airport, I would never have made it. I believe she was an angel. Maybe all the other people who made it possible were angels too!

Poppy flower for remembrance

Genesis 1: 27

So, God created man in his own image, in the image of God he created him; male and female he created them.

Miracles

do happen

The miracle of nature

As I write these words in 2020, we are in the throes of the Corona Virus Pandemic that has struck the world with vicious ferocity. We are in lockdown, being advised to venture out only to buy groceries, have half an hour exercise or travel to essential work.

The month is April and nature is ignoring the chaos and uncertainty. Before our very eyes, she is once again performing her miracles. Whatever is going on with human beings, our births and deaths are of no significance to what's happening in the natural world.

Seeds that had dropped into the earth, months or years ago are now sprouting, pushing their way through the ground, bringing new life. The trees, shrubs and flowers are appearing without fail. Birds are singing and collecting nesting material. Soon the Swallows will arrive.

It's a wonderful world out there. Let's treasure it.

Seeds planted in my life

Many years ago, seeds were planted in my heart during my upbringing as a young Roman Catholic girl. I was indoctrinated within the Catholic church and primary schools to fear God. Once I became an adult, I withdrew from all things religious yet I never lost my belief that God existed.

Sadly, the fear that I had learnt as a child didn't disappear and I was convinced that God must surely have washed his hands of me. There were so many things I felt I had done wrong. I became fearful of dying.

But then my own miracle happened when I came to know God as my loving father. Just as those Poppy seeds that were strewn upon the ground, miraculously emerged as radiant red flowers, the beauty of God's love now shines in my life.

Miracle on the internet

When my sister and I began to research into our family history, we had visited a house where we knew our mother had lived as a child. I gave my phone number to the present owner, encouraging her to call me if she discovered any information that might be useful to us.

A year later she did, in fact, telephone me with news of a visit from an American family but had neglected to gain any contact details from them. We felt these people must be related to us in some way but were devastated that it would be like looking for a needle in a haystack. Over the next few days, my sister frequently prayed to God, "If you want me to find these people, please help me."

One week after that phone call, feeling extremely despondent we inserted the names of our grandparents into a genealogy site and up popped an email address of someone else interested in those people. Within a few minutes, we found that the person with the email address was part of the family that had visited the house in Essex. And yes, they were related to us. We received unexpected answers. It was a miracle on the internet.

Miraculous healing

Stephen, my nephew hadn't been feeling too good and asked his mother to drive him to an appointment at the hospital. His foot was becoming more numb by the minute and as he opened his car door, he found it wouldn't bear his weight. His mother, who was already making her way towards the building turned to see what was delaying her son. He shouted that he couldn't stand up. She quickly returned to his side and assessing his difficulty told him to wait there and she would get someone with a wheelchair. Before they knew what was happening, he was being whisked into emergency treatment as his body slipped into paralysis at an alarming rate.

Many hours of tests followed with an eventual diagnosis of multiple sclerosis. His family were told he would be paralysed for life and there would be little chance of him ever becoming a father. As he was about to marry his Japanese fiancé, this was a major blow. However, Stephen had a tremendous attitude of positivity and soon became adept at manoeuvring his wheelchair in all situations.

He and his bride were married and his new wife quickly had to learn to see to all his basic needs. She even learnt to drive so that they could travel. They moved into an apartment and began their married life in earnest.

With an amazing effort and encouragement from his team of physiotherapists, Stephen began to stand, then walk again. The team couldn't believe what they were seeing. His progress was nothing short of a miracle. But more miracles were to take place. At the time of writing this piece in 2020, Stephen is the proud father of four children. He still has a few problems and is on medication but with no obvious signs.

Another miraculous healing took place in 1988 when my three-year-old son was taken ill with meningitis. He had woken that morning but was listless so I made him comfortable in an armchair while I prepared my older boy for school. As the morning advanced, he remained sleeping where I had lain him earlier. My husband telephoned me at about 11 o'clock and was shocked to hear what was happening at home. I had already telephoned the surgery who informed me that the doctor would make a home visit after his morning surgery.

As soon as the doctor checked my son, he instructed us to get him to hospital as soon as possible. My husband had arrived shortly before the doctor so we wasted no time. Soon we were storming through A & E to the nurses' station who had been warned to expect us. My poor baby, by this time unconscious, was stripped of his clothes to try to bring his temperature down and before long he'd been given an epidural with a strong dose of drugs.

He was in the hospital for fifteen days before being allowed home. He eventually and miraculously regained full health with no side effects.

Finding a sister

When my sister Ronnie and I discovered that we shared our father with a brother and sister, we imagined the task to find them would be almost impossible. If our sister had married, she would have changed her name and they could have moved many times over sixty years. However, we were not to be beaten.

Ronnie found the email address of a man who headed the towns genealogy society. A note to him brought a swift reply that she should contact the local historian by letter as the lady was not on the internet, but interestingly, she had recently had a book about the area published.

We had to wait several days before an envelope coming from Essex dropped through the letterbox.

The historian was so happy to tell us that not only did she know our sister, but Beryl was living in the village next door to the house she had lived in all those years ago with our father. Sadly, our brother had died a few years earlier so we were not to meet him.

A meeting with our sister Beryl was soon arranged. Seeing her for the first time was like looking at our father. It was so uncanny. Wonderfully, there was no bitterness between us. We bonded straight away, exchanging stories of our lives. She was in her 70's, ten years older than Ronnie and seventeen years old than me. What an astonishing discovery after such a length of time.

Everyday miracles

All the miracles I've talked about so far are my personal experiences of miracles, but what about the miracles that happen every day, that we take for granted.

New birth, butterflies and moths developing from caterpillars, an egg maturing into a chick, and the metamorphosis of numerous insects. I could go on, but I hope you get the picture. Miracles are happening every day before our eyes. Maybe we should stop once in a while to wonder at this awesome world we live in.

We are all part of God's miracle

I'm still learning to trust God rather than trying to deal with living my way; to believe that he loves me unconditionally, but when I do trust him, I find that miracles do happen.

Do you know that every single one of you reading these words is loved by our father in heaven? Unconditionally! We are all his children. He knows all about us: our name; the number of hairs on our head; our thoughts; our desires; our needs; our fears. He knows it all.

But he's not a god who is a stone statue or a wooden icon. He is real.

He loves to hear us talk to him.

He wants to converse with us.

He wants a relationship with us.

He loves each one of us so much that he sacrificed his only son, Jesus for us.

Through Jesus, we can reach the very throne room of God. Did you realise that?

Through Jesus, we can reach the very throne room of God. How is that possible?

When Jesus defeated death on the cross, he returned to his father in heaven, but he didn't leave us alone – no, he left his Holy Spirit as our helper on earth. The Holy Spirit is our link to our father God. So how can we get the Holy Spirit to help us? How can we receive help from the Holy Spirit?

We can say a simple prayer, asking Jesus to come into our lives, to fill us with his Holy Spirit, who will provide us with the right words to say, with the right actions to take, and with the right thoughts in our minds.

You might be thinking – I've prayed so hard but God still hasn't answered or done what I've asked of him. Believe me, I've been through many times when my prayers seemed to go unanswered. But I am learning every day, to trust my heavenly father. He knows me so well, that he knows what's best for me. I just have to get my head around it and believe it.

So please, don't think our father has forgotten you, or is punishing you, or has given up on you. No, he is here with you, every step of the way. He is holding your hand. Sometimes he will be carrying you in his arms. Sometimes he will shelter you under his wings, protecting you, loving you.

So, don't despair, learn to trust him; learn to love him as he loves you, his dear child. Ask Jesus to come in and help you with His Holy Spirit.

True miracles indeed!

I hope you've enjoyed reading this book; that you've found it inspiring, that it made you laugh or has given you food for thought.

Thank you for joining me on this journey. Please share the book with your family and tell your friends about it. I'm always grateful for messages on Facebook and Amazon. It's encouraging to hear readers' points of view

About the author

Dee is author of two previous books.

'Unexpected Answers' tells the story of her parents' life-long secret.
'Linked Evermore' is about her great grandfather, a musician who left his family to seek his fortune in America. Both are romantic novels inspired by the lives of real people.

Dee lives in East Sussex at the foot of the South Downs. She loves craftwork, reading, playing the piano and is a leader within Parche, an organization that takes the Christian Gospel into care and retirement homes for the elderly.

Printed in Great Britain
by Amazon

39652752R00075